To All the Yellow Flowers

Previous Publications:

"Diaspora Fragile," "Cantastoria of My Kitchen or My Place on This Earth," "I Saw the Sword of David," and "When Exotic Becomes Side Dish" have all been previously published in *Voices* at Swarthmore College.

"Obstacles to Friendship with God" has been posted on the YouthSpeaks YouTube page for *Brave New Voices 2019*.

For those soon to be whole

Acknowledgments:

- Bitaniya, for the title, and for sticking with me through everything.
- Timothy, for the exquisite and honest illustrations; they reflect your heart.
- Merlino, for your kind words, wisdom, and patience. And the cat pictures.
- Will Giles, for your sharp eyes and giving spirit.
- Auntie Ilyon, for helping me grow.
- Javon Johnson, for your inspiring truth.
- Abby, for all your light. You're one-of-a-kind.
- Sager, for good guitar melodies and better lessons.
- Faith, Hannah, Temba, and Liz, for just being yourselves.
- Khalo Osama, for your vitality and ability to turn anything around … except your dog.
- *Brave New Voices*, for teaching me how freedom feels.
- Bamboo Bistro in Swarthmore, for the egg-drop soup and inspiration.
- Amman, for being my first Philadelphia.
- Seattle, for raising me to love the rain on my windowsill.

To All the Yellow Flowers

Poems by

Raya Tuffaha

Golden Antelope Press
715 E. McPherson
Kirksville, Missouri 63501
2020

Copyright ©2020 by Raya Tuffaha.

Cover Image and Design by Raya Tuffaha and *canva.com*.

Cover finalized by Rusty Nelson.

Interior Drawings ©2020 by Timothy St. Pierre.

Author photo by Ziggy Spiz.

All rights reserved. No portion of this publication may be duplicated in any way without the expressed written consent of the publisher, except in the form of brief excerpts or quotations for review purposes.

ISBN: 978-1-936135-90-5 (1-936135-90-6)

Library of Congress Control Number: 2020933269

Published by:
Golden Antelope Press
715 E. McPherson
Kirksville, Missouri 63501

Available at:
Golden Antelope Press
715 E. McPherson
Kirksville, Missouri, 63501
Phone: (660) 665-0273
http://www.goldenantelope.com
Email: ndelmoni@gmail.com

Foreword by Matthew Merlino

In grad school, the scholar Al Filreis taught me one could fashion a shorthand for the history of American poetry as a story rooted in the figures of Whitman and Dickinson, the expansive public poet, the minimalist poet of privacies, the long, sweeping lines begging to be declaimed, the short lines broken by those enigmatic dashes demanding close textual attention. Such a history is a fiction, like so much history, but at times a useful one. Reading Raya Tuffaha's first collection of poetry, *To All the Yellow Flowers*, I see a powerful young poet dancing gracefully between the traditions and resources offered by these American roots, exploring her world by traveling down both routes.

"Affirmation" begins the collection with four tight Dickinsonian quatrains, and yet even here I hear Whitman in the poem's insistent anaphora. And then to move directly into "First Impressions" could cause whiplash if piloted by a lesser writer. The lines sweep across the page, the voice is public, performing stand-up in the life-or-death setting of America today, Whitmanian with a touch of the Black Mountain school—but Dickinsonian in its mordant humor. To borrow Whitman's old chestnut, Tuffaha's poetry contains multitudes.

But it feels false or forced to tell Raya's story this way, not just because I'm writing it in terms of two white American poets, but also because I can't pretend to have critical or scholarly distance from my own student—not from some competitive MFA program, but from a small, all-girls high school in the Pacific Northwest. I can remember when I first felt the power of Raya's words: a Martin Luther King, Jr. Day assembly organized by our school's Multicultural Student Union, for which Raya performed a spoken word piece that left me shook and inspired, or in Dickinson's words, I felt physically as if the top of my head were taken off.

Raya's spoken word breaks the easily mimicked conventions of the genre, while that physical voice lends its force to these poems on the printed page. When I finally got to work with Raya as a student in my senior English class, I got to know her humor, her passion for social justice, her ability to be an insightful critical voice one moment, a caring friend the next, and a silly teenager a minute later. And I am so impressed that Raya has woven all her voices into the warp and woof of her text. As she writes in "Institutional," "in Chinese class we learn every character / has its own history, so in other words, / in class we learn language makes itself / alive, so in other words / I know my history is alive every time I speak." Raya invites us in to hear from her multiple selves, from selves we too often ignore or silence or simply do not hear, selves we separate and refuse to hear in chorus: teen, woman, Palestinian, student, scholar, activist, American of color, queer, Muslim. Her words ring out with her history, and if we listen well, our own.

—Matthew Merlino

Contents

Acknowledgments	iv
Foreword by Matthew Merlino	v
To All the Yellow Flowers	1
Affirmation	3
First Impressions	4
I Saw the Sword of David	8
Diaspora Fragile	10
Ode to All the Pices Women in My Life	12
College Essay Prompt	13
Things That Make Me Happy	15
Hypnosis	16
Holy	18
Mirror Image	20
الأصفر	23
Should I Love A White Man	26
Lot's Wife	28
Cantastoria of My Kitchen or My Place on This Earth	30
When Exotic Becomes Side Dish	32
Anthem	34
October Sixth	35
Nightmares	37
Institutional	39
More Things That Make Me Happy	43
Scarlet Letter, Abridged	44
Sickness	48

viii CONTENTS

Light Shines Through	49
Ayat Al-Nour (The Verse of Light)	53
Troubled Water	54
Shallow End	57
Cynthia Erivo Plays a Concert at Midnight	58
Should I Love A White Woman	59
The Brown Girl in Seattle Reflects on the Rain	63
Obstacles to Friendship with God	64
My Best Riddles	68
After Javon Johnson: When the Cancer Comes	69
Appendices	**73**
A. Glossary	73
B. "Institutional" with Translations and Pinyin	75
About the Author	**81**

To All the Yellow Flowers

Affirmation

    And so it is and so it will be
    All that I will to be will be
    All that I am is proof of me
    All that I was is in service of what I will be

    I am completely
    made, divinely
    capable, of
    all that came before me

    All I am is enough
    I am all I am is enough
    For I am
    All who came before me

    And so it is.
    And so it is.
    And so it is.
    And so it will be.

First Impressions

I've been trying to write
the perfect identity joke
One that isn't too brash
or wordy or simple
One that leaves pearl necklaces
without needing readjustment;
the kind of witty grin to turn ballrooms
from echo chambers to greenhouses

    Like, I'm not five feet tall but my voice reaches fine
    I was one of five Arabs in my school
    of seven hundred and eleven but that
    just makes me irreplaceable
    "Yea, I went to Catholic school on Friday
    and the mosque on Saturday,
    so you could say I'm God's most devoted
    literary critic."

    Not every joke works, I've learned
I can't say
"Airplane food, am I right?" without worrying

    someone
    will call the FBI
    So I take it slow, take it easy, take
painstaking bites into prickly paradoxes
Like, in this room of glittering
mirrors and sterile glares and rosé
How else can I introduce myself
to you that won't commission you
painting me as the brown one
the loud one, the one with a voice like a bomb
like the feeling of dust in your throat

Raya Tuffaha

Like, do I have to play the game again
the simple tic tac toe of diaspora
the three strikes you're out of the suburbs
                      In this game, I'm allowed to read
                            the rule book blindfolded
In this game, curls can bounce but not frizz
                      Girls can laugh but not rejoice
                Lips can smile, they've got no other choice
In this game, the board isn't level
It's covered in landmines and
all it takes is one roll of the dice
In this game, nothing can be consumed but
                            everything in
                            the room is
                      absolutely palatable

                    I asked my white friend how
                        she gets ready for parties,
She said, "I brush my teeth, shower,
put on a dress and smile."
She said it takes her about ten minutes
                    When I get ready for the same party
                        it takes a little longer:
                            as I brush my teeth,
                                I practice
                          "Hey! How are you?"
                    four hundred and one times
                            in the mirror
                pull out my notes from summers of
speech class taught
by a woman from Atlanta
                    stuff every rolled "r" and cardamom
                    vowel down to the base of my spine

—bound and gagged, they hold me upright
                When I shower for parties I use holy
                      water instead of olive oil
            scrub away at everything dark earth,
      leave pale writhing branches for arms instead
              I practice tying my hair away
                  four hundred and one times

and sometimes the mirror breaks
before I get there
          I always make sure my dress allows me to run
Run all the way home
all the way till I'm knee-deep
                    in Mediterranean waves
and then back again. I make sure I can
            lift my arms all the way up and then
              swing them back down to grab a pen,
writing joke after joke after joke
                      because I'm spinning
               the roulette wheel for a laugh,
playing the game of life again

So at the party my teeth are
brushed and my hair is
washed and my dress is on
and my words swirl around flutes of champagne
while eyes dart for exit signs
             Sometimes, I really smile at the party
              Sometimes I laugh at my own jokes
when they're not too brash or wordy or simple
Sometimes I wish
I wouldn't turn myself into a punchline
wish I wasn't so brash or wordy or simple
I don't know how to spin
my straw hair to golden locks,

       eloquently articulate all the bullshit
     my family has gone through so I could even
be at this damn party
where sterile glares wish
my story would
      magically warp into the perfect identity joke
Sometimes I wish I wore
my hair down more
Pride has never been
something to swallow, to tie
     above your head so you can't see it but
      sometimes I wish people wouldn't
stare at my hair like it holds
the secret to a family riddle
     So I braid my generations of immigrants,
      all the silks and spices,
    all the stories my grandfather told me
      braid them into sea glass
     clench them between sweaty fingers
      until they're smooth one-liners,
     pluck them from the Mediterranean,
      hold the paprika, and serve up
    a masterpiece on a clean white plate

because, you see,
I've been trying to write
a perfect identity joke

I've been trying to write a perfect identity   joke

I Saw the Sword of David

I saw the sword of David
hanging from a wire
in a glass cage
by the Bosporus sea
caught in the light it
glowed
beamed between its bars.
Reminded me of home where
the slats outside the window curve
like a woman's back
keeping old men out and
young girls in, white knuckle clutching at
puffy clouds
and sharp little chins stay high
like hopeful cigarette smoke from the
cab hustler in the street;
in curlicue amen and hallelujah
while the roses in his hand drip blood-
red petals to the gutter.
Home, where they measure your waist
like prime rib from Eden
and casual bites foreign vernacular
academia works in familiar ears, only
language spoken is heard
reaching down the castle steps,
words can cut air sharper than home-cooked meals,
the only keys I hold are those
to the city...
to the castle...
to the sea...
Did the sword gleam without first being spoken to?

Did anyone hear me?

I saw the sword of David, it's true
Leaving Bosporus Bay, I realized
I would have preferred the stone

Diaspora Fragile

After a conversation with George Abraham

There's diaspora in every
    little crevice
        of the world
A community of one in a
    single dandelion
        seed or
shiny new sneakers
on   old school floors
    or fresh pen
    scratches on new
        black tar
    notebook

like lecture hall ink spilled red purple handprints
Hands up don't shoot like that
isn't the path to get to school
    through
checkpoints and barbed wire and
just a stone's throw away

No, no. Not here.

At elite institutions we open the floor
together, open
season, burning tires, us all
burned out

or maybe it's just in
my head, walled in
all of us
together

Maybe diagnosis is a privilege
like pointing at apartheid in textbooks
Shouting here
it is
I can see it, I have
always felt it

I sit in the back
row, fuming at all
the smoke
and mirrors

        while beside the boy from Bethlehem
        who sits
        Quiet
        Smirking or
        serene or
        stunned;
        He is silent, reading
        He leaves

me
        to char the pavement
        and go
        out with a bang

Ode to All the Pices Women in My Life

(Plus That One Male Cousin and That Guy from College,
You Know Who You Are)

Here's to you, the good listeners,
the healers,
the artists and game developers.

Here's to you, musicians, maestros
the preachers and the sermons.

Here's to all the playdates, good days
in all the bad months
you grow with the smallest drop of sun.

Here's to shaking the dust better than Anis,
finding love or heaven or
those principles Danez mentioned.

To tunnel ends and shaky entrances,
minor keys and major setbacks,
grass we wove and stones we threw, here,

Here is to the daydreams and the nights outside
the protests, porch swings, prom-posals,
phone calls and pink hair and photoshoots and pianos,

To the hugs and the garden beds all made,
the watering and the care
here is to you

As you are

to me.

Here's to the path back home
we left in the mud
may we never walk it alone
again.

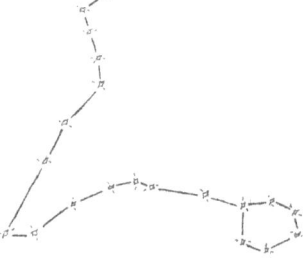

Raya Tuffaha

College Essay Prompt

"If you were to draw a Venn diagram of yourself, how would it look?"

Mine would be an absolute clusterfuck.

There'd be a circle for Arab, a smaller one in that for Palestinian, another one for Muslim, then one for female, then one for queer, then American, then trilingual, then really fucking short, then sister and daughter and cousin and friend and aunt, niece, even Seattleite, maybe one for some kind of mental illness, but Seattle has crazy high depression rates because none of us know what the fucking sun looks like so maybe I don't even need a separate circle for that maybe it's just implied, maybe I don't even need a Seattle—I swear I've seen the sun before. I lived in Jordan

Is there a circle for Jordanian?
All I have of those years are dust-stained shoes and
conversation starters
when I moved back, I lost something in the shipping
Is there a circle for Syrian?
Can I add a circle for a place that only exists
in my grandmother's memory?
Can I draw a circle around the flavors of home; I know
how Syrian spices taste
they taste the same way my grandmother looks at me

as I watch her city grow backwards, crumbling
between dashes of fire and fury
She turns on the stove with a click, click, click, boom,
I drop the bomb:

"Tayta, I got into a college."

she turns from the stove as the spices simmer in the pan
the Venn diagram falls apart, the city
comes crashing down in oily pop pop pop
ruins of something she lives, something I have
yet to learn to miss.

My Venn diagram would be one circle.
Not the sun, not the cooking pan, not
the fire sizzling below.
It would be her
arms around me with a whisper,
"Congratulations."

Raya Tuffaha

Things That Make Me Happy

1. Jokes that don't have a punchline
2. Symmetry
3. Catching my phone right before it hits the ground
4. Candlelight
5. Long lists

Hypnosis

When I snap my fingers, you will fall asleep
One
Two
Three
Lean into the sound of my voice
Lean all the way back into your memory far far

Hold on, you're too far gone
Wait for me, can I ask you to stay?
Hold on, you're falling too far, you're nothing
more than your memory now

Can you hold on
       to the refuge you stole
              from my throat for just long enough
                    to forget
                        why you left me?

Leaning into the sound of my voice like it could echo
                all the way back to where you are

                Do you ever regret falling
            with your eyes open?
      Tell me that
today

you've found your ivory tower,

thrown all your hair down
        its side and   let it tumble

                        to the ground

					Did you ask it to trust
					you first?
													Did it say yes?

When I count to three you will awaken once more

One

Two

Holy

And I'll ask you again: aren't you holy?
This,   you,   now,   here,   how do I pray
    you
give me star-crossed sin again
            won't you?

"Palm to palm is holy palmer's kiss"
Let me learn by the book, you
                make me an altar   for
                  my body
                  a temple

My god, you are   stunning
              if your hands held water,
              there would be no drought
you laugh   like thunderstorms, you are so
    striking
            You make oasis of a wasteland,
      all this
                waste, here

        My god, my body
    hurts
                other people
  have left their marks, I have the scars to prove
    My god,
        my body hurts other people
  swimming upstream, letting current
            love grow stale and wilted
I am hurting so much

    My god, I am
               so lonely
I'm begging you to love

                                        me before you
                        teach me how to love myself
    "A sea nourished with loving tears"

I beg you, my palms together
                teach me
        how
                make me
        whole

Mirror Image

A Palestinian boy from Ramallah is walking home
when a soldier shoots him point blank
and that boy's name was / not Trayvon Martin
                              they both knew
                              the same fear

Four Palestinian kids in Gaza are playing together
            on the beach
when all of them are killed in plain sight
and all those boys' names were / not Tamir Rice
                              they all knew
                              the same fear

A Palestinian in Jerusalem was photographed
            with smiling soldiers
before being dragged to prison where he was tortured
and that Palestinian's name was / not Sandra Bland
                              they both knew
                              the same fear

And Staten Island / isn't Bethlehem
         Minneapolis / isn't Bil'3een
North Charleston / isn't Haifa

but what we see is / what we know, is / not what happened,
   is / nothing, is
            shallow / thin as a textbook page

We march together so they build another checkpoint and hold
            us in the waiting room

Raya Tuffaha

We reach our hands over our heads to climb
out of the hole we're in / they tell us we stand in
our own graves
When they don't feel
gravity, they / confuse falling for flying

We are made / foreigners to our mistakes
human rights / violated
empty jail cells / waiting for us
more relevant
 to the stain / we were born / in than
the situation / they left us

They read our names off laundry lists like / our language
 tastes metallic
They shackle our clenched fists, tell us now / isn't the time
for obstinate tongues
we can't argue / comply / speak truth to covered ears
All we can do is write / a hashtag

Help me, / tell me
how to condense a legacy / of oppression
        to a catchy phrase
to be pasteled and t-shirted and reblogged
something that rhymes / with Mohwtini: my homeland
I Can't Breathe: my right / an inaudible scream
        in the dark

How do you demand your life back
when your backbone is shattered?
How do you pray when God didn't choose you?
How do you ask for anything when your language is torn /
from your throat
bleached and embellished / handed back

America, your core / no cleaner than your ally's

        You both strip / cultures not your own
in fear that you'll realize / this country is not either
Your nations are rooted / in fear / only when you are not
afraid do you
        take the liberty of / assigning justice

America, you spend a whole lot of time afraid / of the
Middle East / So do I

    I don't recognize it / I'm afraid
                I have seen it before
dark-skinned children / never knowing their homes
before being antagonized / in their own stories
                used / for target practice

Do you know how it feels
to never have existed and known / where to locate your home
on a map?
                My home / my country / war-torn and shrouded in
starry banners—

                I am afraid of what it's become

A Palestinian girl from Seattle / was watching the news
                at home
watching armor-clad white / faces march down
                the street
and in one shot / the TV turned into a mirror

الأصفر
For Nader

I became the sun the first day we met; remember,
you told me you loved me in yellow
and I remembered *al-asfar* like
I'd uttered it every morning
Al-asfar, the color of joy and second chances

Before that day, the Arabic language was participation
trophy I carried
between my shoulder blades
Now, I see your face and I want to read Darwish for you
want the world to forget Gibran and think of me instead
to sing until Fairuz's melodic mezzo falls
to the *hawa, ya hawa*
Ya habibi, I see you

first day of orientation with the smooth voice,
Philadelphia August through the windows
illuminating
you, speaking with the grace of
an astrophysicist, vigor of a filmmaker
weaving *qoton* and *harir* words to the room of family:
"I'm gay," you said, "and I know that's accepted here."

Darwish wrote,
"Where can I free myself in the homeland of my body?"
and you moved across the world for school, so confident
in love
foreign soil could grow in you
Brown boy, how do you protect your heart?

Pronounce your name
for me again, you hear

again and again
till the cracks in the pavement wear your soul

I watch you learn to hide and fashion a new American figure
like keeping the Target receipt on the outside of the bag
like holding me telling me it's okay
in English till the far moon rises
I want to know, who held you in Bethlehem?
Have you ever been in love?

There are so many days I want to learn from you
mostly forgiveness, the kind that comes
with freedom, or trust,
or how to cross stitch words from home into the roof
of my mouth
All I want is for you to make a home here,
catch the light at the right time

And I know my Arabic is broken
Your English isn't perfect
but I think we understand each other better
than anyone else

We keep doing the thing where we sit
in the dark and make
all the light ourselves
holding small candles and watching
the flames pirouette or
bending desk lamps into spotlights
We let the rays beam from our teeth
watch the piano keys glisten to the beat of conversation

You're so sure of your questions
I wonder if you left the answers back home

Raya Tuffaha

How do you translate everything
for me?

In which language does "liberation" sound better?
　　　　In Arabic, *tahrir*,　　　　　or in English, rebirth?

Should I Love A White Man:

"My darling," I'd say,
"There are a few things you should know.

One: on our first date,
I locked my heart shut and hoped
the key fit in your palm
        (I mean I hoped it wasn't
        too heavy or brassy)
I waited for you to come find me
        (I mean I hid under the carpet
        and in the corners of the ceiling)
I lay on the ground
        (peeked under the door and I saw your feet)
I watched your shadow
        (pirouette round my fingers)
All this to say I knew you
were there before you did

Two: I hold onto you a lot
        (I mean no disrespect)
Little turns of corners and phrases
        (I mean Arabic is hard to pronounce)
Whispers and murmurs follow me sometimes
        (in your neighborhood, around picket fences)
I hold tight because I don't want to let you go
        (I don't want to go)
All this to say I know you want something
to protect

Three: I talk a lot like a lot a lot it's not a random thing I know I have a lot to say I know I promise I do plenty of people have told me this all I need you to do is listen sometimes just for a little you don't have to like everything you don't have to agree just listen to my story I promise it will be worth it I promise I will be all this to say

    Four: I love when we say nothing at all

Just the two of us
Nothing at all
Just the two of us
Nothing at all
Just the two of us
Nothing at all
Just the two of us
Nothing at all"

Lot's Wife

Before her stands a pillar of salt
Her hands, dripping and void
fumble breath into the structure
and the pillar begins to crumble

She wonders why she falls   for men, every boy
with soft hands and brown curls   she laces
gentle caresses through locks
hoping to click in the right place,   open

Behind her, footprints, overgrown
The base of her spine bereft
boulders tumbling from the hillsides

She remembers everything   that has yet to happen,
walk me home? she pleads,   and of course they say,
lend her an arm, escape

Below her quivers swallowed into earth
making love of lust of course

She falls for men so they won't   hurt her
takes care of others before they take it from her

Above her piece of mine chimes the dove

if she loves every boy too hard forever

there won't be anything left to destroy

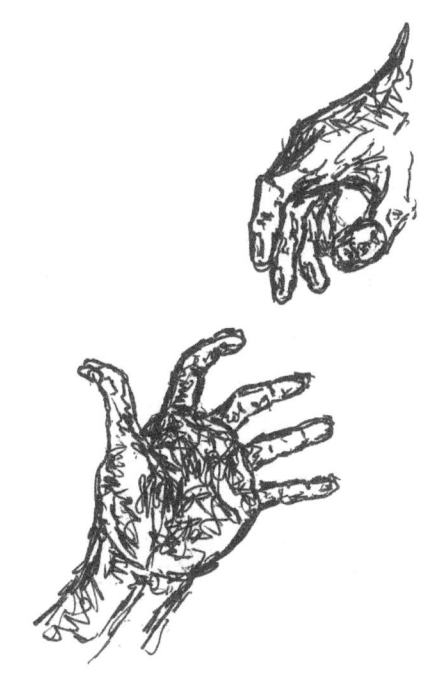

Cantastoria of My Kitchen or My Place on This Earth

Grow, she tells me, from
all the dirty sizzling around me,

the stove
gasoline daughter, don't

you slip through my fingers
oily snap crackle prick one of those

needle-like glances, over-the-counter ease
in the side drawer, medicine cabinet—

Grow, she tells me
from all that has yet to consume

me
a full meal in

years to come,
they will water the sunflowers over my shadow

the backyard garden with basil and lavender:
she used to send me foraging

for the fullest growths,
I would come back

proud hands of harvest and drop
them all in the pan, watch

them sizzling, falling apart at the seams,
the core, rotten

from the oil
from the gasoline

liver exploding in the sear.

Grow, she tells me and

I don't hear the garden outside.
All I smell is gunpowder

burning leaves oily handprints
opening drawers

and I almost slip away again

When Exotic Becomes Side Dish

Becomes cumin over
curiosity baked
saffron new family
recipe to bring
home like a fresh
meeting,becomes
Burned pita bred polite
good girl, *ammoura*,
princess of
the dishes in the
sinking feeling of
coriander fingerprints
on the tablecloth
or between curls on
eyebrows raising
loaves before
guests arrive
Or wrapped in
earthenware for
first hello and thank you for
having me
Then, the temperature
begins to rise.

When spicy becomes
the curve of your back,
cashmere, lace and
tatreez min Ramallah
olive oil glisten to
clinking glasses and
"This is wonderful,"
"What flavor is this, how
do you say it?"
"What language do you
speak at home?"
: how does your tongue
fold
flavor
into the missing parts of
your dinner table
Who wears the pants
after the meal
full belly guffaw;
do you wipe your plate
of femininity, rinse as the
creek
of women flows into the
kitchen;
What language do
the women speak at home?

How do you say it?
: Jasmine nights and
za'atar mornings catch
in between my teeth
dirty fangs bared ready
for the carnage across
the table, there
is no correct answer:
All they see are the
optics and acrobatics,
the men in cologne and
cigarette smoke beards
with their shiny fat belt
buckles on the couch,
arms
extended for the figs and
watermelon
at the table

Raya Tuffaha

All they see is the
watermelon
on the table

Where are the women?
: Cutting the
watermelon, picking
the figs, kneading the
bread, growing the family
home swelling
it with belly
laughs and warm
stories
an inimitable tapestry,
secrets in the coffee pot
the grandest reception
by invitation
only, untranslatable
English, Arabic,
trilling musicality,
under-the-counter
recipes.
What language
do you speak at home?
What is this
flavor called?
How do you say it?
Where are the women?
: I cannot say.
Thank you for
having me.
: I cannot say.
Thank you for having
me.

"Forget your perfect offering
Just ring the bells you still can ring
There is a crack in everything
That's how the light gets in"

-Leonard Cohen, "Anthem"

October Sixth

The water is   in two
         split
One half sleek,
cobalt and gray,
a dark promise,
a façade
                    The other half darker,
                    almost black
                    Waves entangling
                      themselves in
                  each other
                        gasping
                    for
                    air
                       It's a thundering cry   for help,
                       a maligned reaching hand
                       The nails of the waves rake
                    the shore,
                       trying to drag themselves
                       to safety
                       crests are bruised with
                       foam, the   crashing faith
                       Standing spinelessly
and shrieking
                    before
                    furious winds—
        It's a rigged game of endurance
                    wind's hushing masks
                       how the waves scream
                    It pushes and pulls
                       the waves, making
                       a mockery
                       of a marionette
        The water now icy, numb, apathetic

And the wind now deaf

Nightmares

        I don't call them demons, for they are
        never cloaked nor tattered, without
      piercing red eyes
   They are not evil nor obedient, they exist
  outside of everything and everyone,
and they are
not creative;
They dance over my eyebrows and behind
  my earlobes, and
    I've learned to stomach them
      let them fester and rot
        where no one else can
        see them

        I get in bed knowing
      they've made it for me
      that morning,
   too scared to let their stories fall
  from my mouth,

     I don't like to sleep; it's when I am
   most aware
  of my humanity
of the bags under my eyes or
my teeth, rattling like tambourines or
boots splashing in the gutter behind me
faster, faster, turn the corner,
  trip over a pipe and my nose
    breaks clean off my face
      I reach for it, stuff it
       in my pocket, wipe
         my eyes from the mud, try
       desperately
     to pull my ankles from his grasp but
    to no avail it's too late he's got me—

Or maybe my worst fear is being
forgotten
so I take comfort in knowing something
is waiting for me
every night
I refuse to fall
      prey to such minuscule narratives
Watch me grow fangs tonight
sleep with a knife under my head—
      not to kill,
           only to leave a mark, a scent,
              let them come   crawling back for more

Institutional

And yes, explaining to extended family the decision to
study Mandarin in college instead of continuing Arabic
is not easy
for example,

اللغة العربية تقارن الأفعال بناءً على جنس الجمهور

however,

中文根本不连动词

and somehow English allows me to explain

this is just like a fanfare,
percussive and piercing

对于我认识的每个人，声音都太大了

I can't remember how
to speak
all the hills and valleys
crumble in my memory

بلدي موجود فيّ

this is how every good song starts

我的国家在我里面

with line breaks woven accompaniment,

بلدي وأنا على قيد الحياة، هنا، ال

do you know the words

我叫佟瑞育

you've been taught for years

إسمي راية نسيم تفاحة

if I told you
I've been shouting
my name
my whole life,
would you believe me, or would the words

在风中飘走

until

لم تكن موجودة أبداً؟

in Chinese class we learn every character
has its own history, so in other words
in class we learn language makes itself
alive, so in other words
I know my history is alive every time I speak
I speak to know I am alive,
speak English to know you
know I am alive

And isn't it funny how justice is not
synonymous with healing

追求正义会伤害人

colony wounds deeper than graves

السعي وراء الحرية لا يخلو من التكلفة

I study communication
of two of the most powerful empires in history
and all that reflects off my walls are echoes
of "why don't you just take French?"

الرومانسية ليست أجمل من عشيقها

doctored generations of literature comparison,
they don't understand

他们都不懂

إنهم لا يفهمون

learning a language aside from your own becomes defiance
sends old ideas of refinement to the guillotine
to the colonizer it says

Raya Tuffaha

我真厉害

watch me cross every bridge you tried to burn

أنت لست مستعدة لثورتي

I know my name in three languages and who are you

إن لم يكن وعد فارغ

to pronounce every one incorrectly

我从来不需要你或你的不相关的词

And I call myself an un-hopeless unromantic

التاريخ لن يكون لطيفا معك

再试一次

to the colonizer

هذه اللغة تعرف كيفية إحياء نفسها

it says

我们不一样

I know where my home is because I'm not afraid to leave it says I'm not afraid to leave it

أنا قوية، حياتي تستحق كل دقيقة أقضي التحدث

to the colonizer it says

什么时候殖民化与教育意义相同?

if you want to break me, you must put me
with my words together first

我挑战你

you cannot break me

مرة أخرى، هل تراثك فخور الكفاية؟

I am not broken

尝试再次打破我

to the colonizer, broken language

لا يحتاج أي شخص إلا نفسه

says I know home will wait for me

告诉我:我还没找到自己

says it is indestructible

我不怕，不能怕

says I am indestructible

ما زلت على قيد الحياة

says I am here

我

在

这

里

أنا موجودة
أنا موجودة
أنا موجودة

More Things That Make Me Happy

1. Julie Andrews' voice
2. Shrimp dumplings
3. The kuffiyeh you let me keep
4. Fresh-oiled curls in the sun
5. Riding in the back of a pickup truck and singing off-key
6. Singing on-key
7. Jokes that make sense in two languages
8. Stargazing
9. The doorknob creaking like it used to
10. Good Old-Fashioned Lover Boy by Queen
11. The smell of orange and ginger
12. You, crossing your knees in a too-small chair
13. You, asking why
14. Water lilies, and sunflowers too

Scarlet Letter, Abridged

>THE DAY I FILED A SEXUAL HARASSMENT CLAIM
>AFTER
>FIVE SILENT YEARS:
>I hid in the back of the school chapel during sixth period
>tears streaming down my face
>voice rising through the rafters
>   into the pounding organ
>and all I could say was
>   [thank you]
>On the other line, the principal stuttered
>and gasped
>and all I could say was
>   [thank you]

Every other word of mine lay between my hip bones, cradled
in the adrenaline that comes with urgency

>   [thank you], I said
>for listening to me
>The principal said [of course], said [I'm so sorry]
>And all I could say
>   I didn't

>   I SAT THERE   instead, white
>   knuckles at Mary's feet
>   REMEMBERING   all the times
>all I could say was
>   "I'm sorry."

"I'm sorry I
- wore this dress today"
- left myself [alone] with [YOU]"
- questioned [YOU]"

In the first ninety seconds [of my phone call],

I APOLOGIZED   six times

On my way back to class,

I HEARD [YOUR] FOOTSTEPS BEHIND ME;   in bed

that evening,
his Georgia drawl droned in my memory:
"How are you, Miss Raya?"
"I hope you're doing well."
"You know you're a special girl."

I didn't sleep that night [counted my heartbeats instead],
felt the fire surge in my lungs
I brushed my teeth [could still taste the guilt]

So dear   [YOU]
If I could go back,
find myself

BEFORE I EVER MET [YOU],

it would take an eternity
[YOU] don't know how long five [silent] years are,
how culpability scalds [your] throat
till voice is all ash;
I was fourteen.
     I was fourteen.
         I was fourteen.
     I was fourteen.
I WAS FOURTEEN

Following me into parking lots and back corners
of the theater:
what did [YOU] want from me?

So, dear   [YOU],

I REMEMBER [YOU]

are the man who taught me to wear red
leave scarlet letter footprints in [YOUR] shadow and
apologize for the mess

I TRANSFERRED HIGH SCHOOLS TO ESCAPE [YOU]

and I only admitted this at the end of my senior year
Do [YOU] know what that is:
for shame to claw its way up your skirt
and into your mind?
Do [YOU] know
what that is:
to bite your tongue till it bleeds scarlet liability;
Do [YOU] know
how to say thank you?

When someone bares their
soul onstage for [YOU],
        do [YOU] say thank you?
Do [YOU] say anything at all?
Or do [YOU] touch her instead?
Trace adolescent curves under [YOUR] grimy fingernails
   as
[YOU] stun her,
swear her to shame and secrecy;
what are [YOU] searching for?

I COULD CALL [YOU] ALL KINDS OF NAMES
but that would give [YOU] more to hide behind

I COULD BEAT [YOU]
but that would let [YOUR] skin near mine again

I COULD SPIT YOUR NAME
but I'd have to clean up the blood

I COULD HATE [YOU].
I COULD HATE [YOU]
but that would make [YOU] worth thinking about

So instead I'll cradle my words [between my hip bones]
feel the flames searing the insides of my cheeks
unclench my fists from Mary's feet
rise
leave the chapel with a whispered [hallelujah]

Someday I'll learn just how holy my body is,
and finally clear [the red from] my name
Someday [YOU] will hear this poem
or I'll pass [YOU] on the street
or we'll end up [in a theater] together [again]
        and [YOU] will forget
    [YOU] will reach for my [hand] again
call me [special] again
ask, "How are you, Miss Raya?" again
and I'll say   I'm sorry   for you

Sickness

Doctor, I've fallen deathly quiet / I'm coughing up acid and / swallowing pride / I don't feel / well today (haven't felt today) / My teeth are / melting my hair (is falling out) / I shattered my kneecaps / last week

and I walked / here alone / crown in my hands / and

isn't that a sickness? / How far does your stethoscope reach (how much of my heart does it hear?)

How far can you pull me / before you hear me break / Doesn't it spread you too thin / to love / the broken nails and hardwood floors of the years?

Caught in a car door or between a rock and a bad dream / so blissfully aching for something / you can't have

a single clue / where my voice has gone / you couldn't possibly understand / could you? can you

put me back together? / Have you sworn to protect anyone? / Have you any heart or idea / how

do you hear me / now / pleading like / I used to, / you're used to that now?

Is this a sickness you can cure or are you here to watch me ask you for help?

Have you ever considered the reason / they don't call you patient? / It can't be because they chose not to / When all their teeth have been corroded,

what's left other than the word help

Raya Tuffaha

Light Shines Through

True story: in the same hour I was misdiagnosed
                                    with BPD,
I texted the first girl I ever had a real crush on
so I guess I've always found myself
in the taboo of something that knows its place
under the rug.

In my house I stand   out a little:
I have a thing for blue lipstick and jokes in languages
no one else speaks
I like ice cream no one in my family will try, like
ube, Mung bean,
green tea mixed with peanut butter cups
or even, sometimes, at the corner of her mouth

Sometimes I hide
the smile at the corner of my mouth when
she calls me beautiful, other times
I tell her not here and
                    wait till dark
to ask for her forgiveness
                    I can't tell you
the number of
nights I've spent
                carving
wishes into the walls
Wallflower, no roots on crumbling brick

She calls me at one
                in the morning
her voice   proud   and   breaking,
"You made it to tomorrow again," breaking
 me
  out of my mind
the panic attack stops.

And an hour before dawn

I begin to understand why queerness was classified as a
mental illness for so long

So tell me
why something so visceral
hurts so shallow it burns under your skin
Why
I didn't tell my parents
      I had BPD until my slam team
      told me they loved me
 and I had etched her name
 into the side of my mind
Borderline personality disorder:
characterized by manic mood swings,
intense aggression, and
the constant feeling that living
      behind a mask
might be the reason you're so
angry all the damn time

My sister calls me lazy, tells me
   I ruin everything.
   I yell at my family
I've seen my dad javelin a fork
    across the w h o l e k i t c hen,
throw his car keys at my feet and force me to
pick them up
My mom asks why
     I don't tell her how I'm feeling
and I hold broken glass to the light
       In moments like those
I'm not sure
  if my hands
ache from holding
    something glass
     or something broken
or something
    that still lets the light shine through

Some days I watch the foundation of my house
rot and I cough up my heart
    My sister says
the week I came out was the worst week
    of her life
    When I heard that, I understood   why
I'm so afraid of being so
fucking angry   all the time
    I cannot allow myself   to invalidate

Example: the fact I   avoid therapy is
not necessarily the reason
    I am afraid of
    running my fingers through her   hair;
Example:
the fact that I am afraid of running
    my fingers through her hair
is not necessarily the reason I avoid   therapy
No, I am afraid of being contagion or being caught
I am afraid of all the trauma it took for someone to build
a shield and call it diagnosis
I am afraid of hurting
her
pulling too hard
asking too quickly
knowing
       too much or nothing at all

I don't want her
               to ever meet my parents
I'm scared of what they won't say
           I want to protect her
from the broken parts of my home
           myself
I want to build   her
           a home
   Living in
some kind of borderline means using glass
   shards to   break

out of my mask,
    putting on my face before I go
      to sleep
Being out in my family means I never fully close my eyes
so my question is
              between borderline and queerness
which is an illness, and which isn't terminal?

I ask her this
at one in the morning
and she says neither are true
She holds her breath with me,
says, "Empty your hands.
Let go."
She tells me I made it to tomorrow
and that's enough for today
We make plans for ice cream at dusk
A soft smile folds over my mouth as
I trace her name on the wall
and watch the sun
              rise over my rooftop
Again

Ayat Al-Nour (The Verse of Light)

اللَّهُ نُورُ السَّمَاوَاتِ وَالْأَرْضِ مَثَلُ نُورِهِ
كَمِشْكَاةٍ فِيهَا مِصْبَاحٌ الْمِصْبَاحُ فِي زُجَاجَةٍ
الزُّجَاجَةُ كَأَنَّهَا كَوْكَبٌ دُرِّيٌّ يُوقَدُ مِن شَجَرَةٍ
مُبَارَكَةٍ زَيْتُونِةٍ لَّا شَرْقِيَّةٍ وَلَا غَرْبِيَّةٍ يَكَادُ زَيْتُهَا
يُضِيءُ وَلَوْ لَمْ تَمْسَسْهُ نَارٌ نُّورٌ عَلَى نُورٍ يَهْدِي
اللَّهُ لِنُورِهِ مَن يَشَاءُ وَيَضْرِبُ اللَّهُ الْأَمْثَالَ
لِلَّهِ بِكُلِّ شَيْءٍ عَلِيمٌ

"God is the Light of the heavens and the earth; the likeness of His light is as a niche within which is a lamp, the lamp is within glass, the glass is as if it were a brightly shining star, lit from a blessed olive-tree, neither eastern nor western, whose oil would almost glow even if untouched by fire—light upon light—God guides to His light whom He pleases, and God presents examples for the people, and God is Knowing of all things."

-Quran 24:35

Troubled Water

    I was supposed to be your rock
    I wasn't meant to   envelop, I'm not that way
    I'm more tether than lifeboat, so

    I'm holding you, bracing
    over the edge   above a roaring river, icy
    metal stanchions grating against my sternum
    I'm clenching
    your wrists till they wail   white, drip
    like the foam hissing at your dangling toes,
    I will never let you go

    And you hear the river screeching
    your name,   I'm sorry,
    I wasn't meant to envelop
    you like your lover does
    No, I don't know how to drink
    like I'll never swim again

    And you cry amber tears,   "the river needs me"
    selfish moans shatter over glistening boulders
    I forgot, your lover taught
    you   the siren's song
    She still beckons somewhere
    deep in your eyes, I know
    She's there when I'm not

    My words rush through your head
    like she's carved a canal for them
    "Don't let go, my darling"
    Does your name taste different in my mouth?
    Does it taste like her?

    I've seen you go back
    and forth, and forward
    and collapse   in my trembling arms;
    when will I know how that feels?

When will you envelop me
the way she always does for you?
Your escapes are so   understanding,
She welcomes you back, every sip   consuming,
makes the undertow a cradle

and my bed is half empty again.
There is something so beautifully human
about the way
two sleeping people hold each other:

not conscious   enough to know
they're breathing, yet
aware
of each other's bodies, giving and taking
pushing and pulling, dreaming in the tide
connecting
one shore to the other:

when will I ever hold
you, my ground,
unafraid of the current below

When will you learn this
is not just about you
It's not about you it's about the river
you're not the river
It's not about the river, no, it's not her
it's me
I need you
now, I need you
right now, I need you, how
can you be so fucking selfish?

This is not about you or the alcohol
This is not about you
This is about me
This is about me
This is not about me being selfish

This is not about you
This is not about you
This is you
This is not about me
This is not about me
This is not me
This is not you
Is it?

Is this you?
Then what am I?
A bridge?

Shallow End

> From the underbelly of the shallow end
> I pulled a lavender stone
> Lumpy and dented—
> no larger than my big toe or my eye
> Eroded and glistening for attention—
> the only pastel on the beach, she was.
> In the center spiraled a supernova,
> white and gold spider arms
> exploding from her hurricane's center—that calm twinkle
> reaching for
> the edges of the shore
> And before the discerning audience of sun rays
> and larger rocks
> and the blue blue cradle which gave her birth
> I held her to my heart
> Here was earth in my palm
> Here, was proof of something to come

Cynthia Erivo Plays a Concert at Midnight

Cobalt windows shadow like
    carpets dirty clothes
    hold secrets
    little messages in the twinkling
    of mirrors, like that.

Stacked desk, empty bag like
    full nights on hour long
    commutes, soprano piano melody asking
    is there more than
    bus rides before the sunrise
    to wake up for?

So far from home, she calls me
    hiding in my bed
    between the blue
    on paper, call them fault lines

Call them breadcrumbs and maybe
    this morning I will find myself
    holding on to anything
    worth holding onto

Should I Love A White Woman

"My dear," I'd say,
        "There are some things you should know.

One: on our first date, I bought you
        a whole garden,
ran my fingers
        through the rosebushes and danced
      them round the daffodils
          I carried it to your door but I could not
            put it down
My hands were covered in mud, laced in
        crimson kisses from thorns
        and so I didn't knock
      grass clippings under my boots and
      oak leaves in my hair,
        I waited for you to come find me
On our second date, I wore my hair down,
watched a grin
        tickle the corners of your mouth
          as your fingers ran through it in
      round robin curlicues;
            I remembered how
to shake your hand instead of holding it,
      My hair knows
        curiosity better than sincerity, clumsiness
        better than malice
          has toyed with cigarette
      smoke and mud and banter and beatings

—

  I did not remember to tell you this
I forgot a lot that night

Two: holding your hand in public is
       like staring down
          the barrel of an unloaded gun
                    With your arm around me,
     every Beverly in these Hills used to grind
                          her teeth how
     gravel crunches under hiking boots
                   All their needling tongues
                       and pointed stiletto nails
        and glares snagged
        in my curls,
    whispers and murmurs of something
        shattered, that's what followed
              me
Sometimes I wondered if you heard it
    until one evening, wrapping
                  me in a blanket, you told me
it was just white noise

Three: a year into our relationship,
    I forgot to mention your name to my sister
Between the trial scene at the end
        of *Legally Blonde* and
        a bowl of tortilla chips,
            your dimples and blue eyes slipped
                my mind
        Between my sister and me, you were
    never there
        In the late-night *qahwa* rounds
            where you leaned into me
and I translated between caffeinated kisses,
        those nights taught me the tightrope dance
      and how to settle for just enough

Four: when you giggled that time
            I asked you to walk me three blocks,
              I became the lamppost you were

            leaning against
When you left me
     to walk alone, one man called me
                             his hot chocolate
                 burned his tongue
     Another grabbed at my arms till
my wrists unscrewed
                 Another took my mouth from right
          under my nose
                       One kept my eyes in his
           pocket and another
cut all my hair from my head
                 When you came to find me, I could not
          call your name
I had forgotten it

Five: my love, sometimes I forget
                               you are mine
         When the world goes to sleep,
         I tuck you in and
                     slip into the shadows,
     walk late nights alone, humming Fairuz
               On our wedding day, I will drape
myself in the purest white silk I can find
         On that day, I will take your hands
                       in mine,
     trace the constellations
                         in your gaze from
underneath my veil
         and remember everything I never told you."

Raya Tuffaha

The brown girl in Seattle reflects on the rain

How many colors can't we see?
Is one of them beautiful like me?
Do they tremor in the crook
of their hideaway nook?
Is quiet all color can be?

If the laws of physics are true,
wouldn't light absorb me too?
Unless my heart doesn't float
so light glimmers and glows
and leaves my skin the residue

How silent must rain patters fall
for someone to feel them at all?
In each little drop
is a color forgot
by begrudging autumn's crawl

How many colors won't I know?
They're all trapped under puddles, though
from the mud under feet
pulsing patient orphaned beats
something beautiful too might grow.

Obstacles to Friendship with God

Dear God, she was beautiful:
Fifteen-year-old me sitting in the very back row
of a sweaty New York theater
watching Cynthia Erivo sing just for me,
her voice taking mine for a waltz,
She was beautiful,
she was powerful,
     and I should have known.

Dear God, she was beautiful:
Sixteen-year-old me sitting in the front row
of the classroom,
with my friend whose blue eyes were
brighter than her smile,
She was beautiful,
she was powerful,
     and I should have known.

I should've known:
the lump in my throat when I had to leave the theater,
when the distance between my friend
   and I went from a weekend to 2,472 miles,
it meant I was losing more than I thought I was,
she wouldn't be there to answer
the question I didn't know I had:
       who am I?

Dear God, you remember that day like I do:
the humid July morning in Washington DC,
the over-salted hotel French toast,
the parent reprimanding her child at the next table.
You remember my ribs clutching at each other in fear,
throat filled with ash, palms baptized in sweat,
and you remember the day
      I came out to my mom.

You remember how I burst into tears
    just as the waitress arrived with orange juice,
and how my lipstick stained the napkin
You remember that day like I do
and I will never forget that day because
she asked me with the most innocent
poison dripping   from her lips:
    "So, do you still consider yourself a Muslim?"
And God, for all my appall I couldn't
    answer the question.
I could smell the smoke but you took
    the color red from my sight,
so I walked on ice with shattered breath:
                              dear God,
Was our friendship ever in question?
Were you ever my friend?
If you created me in your image,
                      why can't I recognize myself?

Dear God, queer youth are thirteen
    times more likely to develop an anxiety disorder.
Is that one time for every year I thought there was
                    something wrong with me?
Dear God, queer youth are thirteen
    times more likely to develop depression.
Is that one time for every year I thought
                    I'd fragmented my culture?

Dear God, what kind of a friend shatters my breath?
And should I even consider myself Muslim anymore
    when this drowning is anything but
                        peaceful?
It's not that I know I am wrong, it's that you will never
    tell me I'm right
Dear God, sometimes I wonder if this world
    and I were meant for each other.

God, you have ninety-nine names

and the first one is Al-Rahman: *compassionate*
The second is Al-Raheem: *merciful*
    What number is protector?
    What number is provider?
    What number is explainer or teacher or refuge?
Dear God, can I not go to you
                for existing in some kind of sin?
Can you forgive yourself for forgiving me?
Did you not create what I hope you won't
                despise?

God, are you there?
Don't you remember me, the girl with the last
                name "apple?"
You gave me the strength of that damn apple in Eden
You let my mother name me Raya
    without letting her realize
                my name means "pride."
You trapped me in this vicious joke
    locked the key in my kiss.
On this humid July morning in Washington DC,
fighting my own revolution in sight of the Capitol building,
    I think I might be your only mistake.
Dear God, I don't think I was meant for this world;
                why won't you let me leave?

Dear God, I know I am shattered like my breath,
but there are people there to pick up the pieces:
Faith, Zaina, Liz, Bitaniya, Lynn, Azura, Halle, Becca, Zivia,
Izzy, Abby, Rachel, Helen—
    they're my better thirteen reasons why not.
They collect my fragments, hold them to your light,
                and read my story from the shadows.
They are beautiful,
they are powerful,
                and I should have known:

       You gave me the people who know I am greater than the
                sum of my shattered parts.

They are the answer to my questions.

Dear God, their friendship,
our friendship, is an anomaly,
built to endure life and death,
                        inside and out.

My Best Riddles

1. how the first mountain climbers finally made it to the summit and found the meeting had just ended
2. those bruises that magically appear on my legs
3. trapped in the glass jar on my desk
4. us, singing This Little Light of Mine
5. other people, sometimes
6. yellow roses on the kitchen table
     they lean on each other
        after all of them have been uprooted

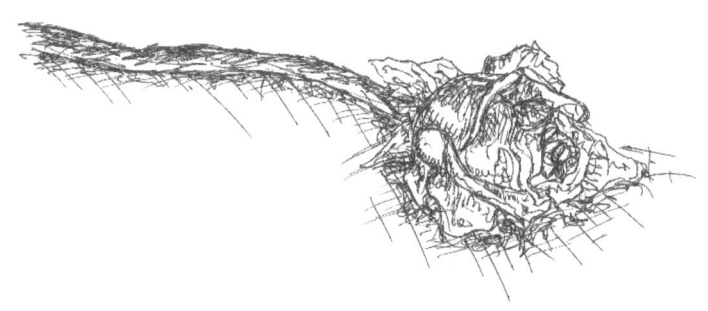

After Javon Johnson: When the Cancer Comes

My uncle Fuad was someone I never remember
speaking to
                      grew up looking at old photos
                          and hearing his stories
When he died, I didn't cry;
an eighty-five-year-old man can only battle
cancer for so long...
but he was

eighty-five in 2019
                      means he was born in 1934
            means he remembered when Palestine
                            was all Palestine
                remembered his country before
                          the cancer came,
bombing living cells into submission and terror,

Amo Fuad had six college degrees and somehow
never learned
                            to live forever,
            to survive dying from the inside out

                He taught generation after generation
                            to grow loud,
        fought cancer by dousing it in olive oil
                    and marching on Fridays
"From the river to the sea," taught them to swim
                              in a dust storm

                They said Fuad was a scholar, a teacher,
                                a great man
              an architect of a liberated future
I can only believe the stories empty buildings tell

                Now, when family regales me with his legacy,
                    how he loved good stories over
                        good coffee with good people,

I wonder how much of someone's
story dies with them,
wonder what he wished I knew
or what he forgot to tell me

My country was someone I never remember speaking to
                              grew up looking at old photos
                              and hearing her stories
Now I'm watching her die, choke
on tear gas and dust,
watch her inside bleed demolition
and conquest—
cells eating each other alive
A millennia old country can only battle
cancer for so long

When someone dies, their family
praises their legacy,
gathers under the shade of an olive tree
to recite *surah at-teen*
Who will *dabke* on Land Day if everyone
has suffocated and the ground
no longer beats?
If I come back to the village
kiss auntie cheeks drink uncle tea
and watch conversation zip past my tongue
too fast for me
to respond, too fast until the
Silence

    the look
    of anticipation

        family
waiting for the mother tongue
        to quit oversleeping

Silence

as she stays in bed

and I ask
in English instead,
"Can you say that again?"
Will there be funeral for my language or theirs?
Little graveyard on my tongue;
I can only believe the stories empty mouths tell

> A month before he died, Amo Fuad
> published a book of our family tree
> his way of ensuring my roots
> ran deeper
> than I'd ever understand
> curled "*bi harf al-daad*"—a language wrapped
> around my throat—
> into the terracotta of his backyard
> in Jerusalem, a city so alive and proud
> it burns with the tick of survival

Late last night, a friend asked if ever
    I thought Palestine would be free

                    and I didn't   say no

I felt my jaw swing wide,
tongue unearth

and I tried to explain how
as indigenous people to Palestinian land, we
    must always live where our country cannot,
        become her
    when she cannot
look death in the eye and say not today,
battle cancer with every living thing left
in a war-ravaged body
        like Fuad
    we all are
dying from the inside out

sick, crumbling, and
for some godly reason, full
of faith in the future

When doors to empty buildings swing
wide open
and the dust settles inside
we march to leave
our footprints at the door

When family trees bear olives,
rupture the sunbeams and entwine
home in their fists
we march, we march, keeping
him
keeping her
between our ribs
Fuad: name, meaning heart.
Meaning beating.
Meaning alive.

Appendices

A. Glossary

Al-asfar — yellow

Ammoura — cute girl, sweet girl, darling

Amo — paternal uncle

"Bi harf al-daad" — "of the letter daad;" Arabic speakers across the Southwest Asia/North Africa region are united by a language that includes an aspirated "d" sound (ض).

Dabke — Palestinian folk dance

Harir — silk

Hawa, ya hawa — "lover, oh, lover" or "wind, oh, wind." Lyric from the Fairuz song Nassam Alayna El Hawa.

Kuffiyeh — traditional Palestinian black-and-white scarf

Qahwa — coffee

Qoton — Cotton

Surah at-teen

> A chapter of the Qur'an that begins, "By the fig and the olive, and by Mount Sinai, and by this secure city, we have certainly created man in the best stature," noting the holiness of these crops and their fertility as well as their affirmation of existence, both of themselves and God.

Tahrir

> liberation

Tatreez min Ramallah

> "hand embroidery from Ramallah;" each city in Palestine has its own distinct style. Tatreez is a highly respected craft entrusted to the older women in the village.

Tayta

> grandma

Ya habibi

> "oh, my sweetheart"

Za'atar

> traditional Palestinian spice mix of thyme, oregano, marjoram, sesame seeds, and olive oil

B. "Institutional" with Translations and Pinyin

And yes, explaining to extended family the decision to
study Mandarin in college
instead of continuing Arabic
is not easy
for example,

اللغة العربية تقارن الأفعال بناءً على جنس الجمهور
*The Arabic language conjugates words depending on the
gender of the audience*

however,

中文根本不连动词
Zhōngwén gēnběn bù lián dōngcí
The Chinese language does not conjugate verbs at all

and somehow English allows me to explain

this is just like a fanfare,
percussive and piercing

对于我认识的每个人，声音都太大了
Duìyú wǒ rènshì de měi ge rén, shēngyīn dōu tài dà le
The sound is too loud for anyone I know to understand

I can't remember how
to speak
all the hills and valleys
crumble in my memory

بلدي موجود فيّ
My country exists in me

this is how every good song starts

我的国家在我里面
Wǒ de guójiā zài wǒ lǐmiàn
My country exists in me

with line breaks woven accompaniment

بلدي وأنا على قيد الحياة، هنا، الآن
My country and I are alive, here, now

do you know the words

我叫佟瑞育
Wǒ jiào Tóng Ruì Yù
My name is Tóng Ruì Yù (Raya Tuffaha)

you've been taught for years

إسمي راية نسيم تفاحة
My name is Raya Naseem Tuffaha

if I told you
I've been shouting
my name
my whole life,
would you believe me, or would the words

在风中飘走
zài fēng zhōng piāo zǒu
drift away in the wind

until

لم تكن موجودة ابدا؟
they never existed at all?

In Chinese class we learn every character
has its own history, so in other words
in class we learn language makes itself
alive, so in other words
I know my history is alive every time I speak
I speak to know I am alive,
speak English to know you
know I am alive

And isn't it funny how justice is not
synonymous with healing

追求正义会伤害人
Zhuīqiú zhèngyì huì shānghài rén
The pursuit of justice can hurt people

colony wounds deeper than graves

السعي وراء الحرية لا يخلو من التكلفة
The pursuit of freedom is never without cost

I study communication
of two of the most powerful empires in history
and all that reflects off my walls are echoes
of "why don't you just take French?"

الرومانسية ليست أجمل من عشيقها
Romance is no more beautiful than its lover

doctored generations of literature comparison,
they don't understand

他们都不懂
Tāmen dōu bù dǒng
None of them understand

إنهم لا يفهمون
They don't understand

learning a language aside from your own becomes defiance
sends old ideas of refinement to the guillotine
to the colonizer it says

我真厉害
Wǒ zhēn lìhai
I am incredible

watch me cross every bridge you tried to burn

أنت لست مستعدة لثورتي
You are not ready for my revolution

I know my name in three languages and who are you
إن لم يكن وعد فارغ
if not an empty promise
to pronounce every one incorrectly

我从来不需要你或你的不相关的词
Wǒ cónglái bù xūyào nǐ huò nǐ de bù xiāngguān de cí
I have never needed you or your empty words

And I call myself an un-hopeless unromantic
التاريخ لن يكون لطيفا معك
History will not be kind to you

再试一次
Zài shì yí cì
Try again

to the colonizer
هذه اللغة تعرف كيفية إحياء نفسها
This language knows how to revive itself

it says

我们不一样
Wǒmen bù yíyàng
We are not the same

I know where my home is because I'm not afraid to
leave it says I'm not afraid to leave it
أنا قوية، حياتي تستحق كل دقيقة أقضي التحدث
I am strong, my life is worth every minute I spend
speaking

to the colonizer it says

什么时殖民化度与教育意义相同?
Shénme shíhòu zhímínhuà yǔ jiàoyù yìyì xiāngtóng?
When did colonialism mean the same as education?

if you want to break me, you must put me
with my words together first

我挑战你
Wǒ tiǎozhàn nǐ
I dare you

you cannot break me

مرة أخرى، هل تراثك فخور الكفاية؟
again, is your heritage proud enough?

I am not broken

尝试再次打破我
Chángshì zàicì dǎpò wǒ
Try to break me again

to the colonizer, broken language

لا يحتاج أي شخص إلا نفسه
does not need anyone but itself,

says I know home will wait for me

告诉我: 我还没找到自己
Gàosù wǒ: wǒ hái méi zhǎodào zìjǐ
Tell me: I haven't found myself

says it is indestructible

我不怕，不能怕
Wǒ bú pà, bù néng pà
I am not afraid, I cannot be afraid

says I am indestructible

ما زلت على قيد الحياة
I'm still alive

says I am here

我在这里
Wǒ zài zhèlǐ
I am here

أنا موجودة
I am here
أنا موجودة
I am here
أنا موجودة
I am here

About the Author

Raya Tuffaha is a Palestinian, Jordanian, and Syrian poet, musician, and activist from Seattle, WA. Currently a student at Swarthmore College, she is a firm believer in artistic liberation and healing through community. Tuffaha most recently published a series in *Voices*, a Swarthmore literary newsletter. In 2019, she helped make Seattle history, placing Team Seattle third internationally during the *Brave New Voices* tournament. She hopes this collection might act as a mirror for someone else to see their own light. When not busy writing, Tuffaha enjoys singing everything from rock to opera, switching languages mid-sentence, and speaking about herself in the third person. She plans on living in New York City and has serious intention of getting a cat.

www.ingramcontent.com/pod-product-compliance
Lightning Source LLC
Chambersburg PA
CBHW062035120526
44592CB00036B/2144